Black Sketchbooks

London · Adam & Charles Black

PUBLISHED BY
A. & C. BLACK · SOHO SQUARE · LONDON W.

✤DURHAM✤

THE CLOISTERS

A·SKETCH-BOOK·BY

Robert J. S. Bertram

A·&·C·BLACK·L^{TD}·SOHO SQVARE·LONDON·1920

THE NORTH AISLE.

THE ·GALILEE·

THE NAVE

CENTRAL TOWER FROM PALACE GREEN.

THE ABBEY GATE

THE CATHEDRAL FROM THE WEST

BISHOP·COSIN'S·DOORWAY·
THE·CASTLE·

THE GREAT HALL OF THE CASTLE.

COURTYARD AND CHAPEL
THE CASTLE

THE · NORMAN · CHAPEL · THE · CASTLE

THE·BLACK·STAIRCASE·IN·THE·CASTLE.

DURHAM FROM THE BATTERY

THE CASTLE AND ST MARGARET'S CHURCH FROM CROSSGATE

FRAMWELLGATE BRIDGE.

FROM THE CASTLE BATTLEMENTS

SADLER·STREET·

THE·MARKET·PLACE

SAINT·GILES'·CHURCH

CLYST BRIDGE

SAINT·OSWALD'S·CHURCH·

NORTH·BAILEY·&·ST·MARY'S·CHURCH·

PREBENDS BRIDGE